JESUS: THE REIGNING KING

A GUIDE FOR FAMILY WORSHIP

BY RICHARD ROSS AND ROB RIENOW

Jesus: The Reigning King

© 2014 Robert Rienow and Richard Ross

ISBN 9781497471818

An offering of worship to Jesus -
the Risen, Reigning, and Righteous King

TABLE OF CONTENTS

INTRODUCTION

WHAT IS FAMILY WORSHIP?

Family worship is when a family gathers together at home for prayer, Bible reading, and turning their hearts to the Lord.

In Deuteronomy 6:5–7 (ESV) we find what Jesus called "the first and greatest commandment":

> *You shall love the LORD your God with all your heart and with all your soul and with all your might. And these words that I command you today shall be on your heart. You shall teach them diligently to your children, and shall talk of them when you sit in your house.*

Immediately after the Great Commandment, parents are called to impress the hearts of their children with a love for God. How can we as sinful parents possibly do this? God tells us to begin with family worship, talking as a family about God and His Word.

God calls us to family worship for many reasons.

- Family worship gives God the honor He deserves in our homes.

- Family worship deepens and strengthens our relationships.

- Family worship provides an opportunity for parents to take the lead in passing their faith to their children.

- Family worship affords a regular opportunity to confess our sins together.

- Families that worship at home bring that spirit of worship into the church.

START SLOWLY

Unfortunately, few Christian adults today grew up in homes that practiced family worship. You probably did not have family worship modeled for you growing up, and, if you are like most Christian families today, it has not been a regular part of your life. There is good news! It is never too late to begin family worship—with teenagers or even grandchildren. It is OK to start slowly.

THIS BOOKLET

This guide will help you prepare a special week for your family, as you intentionally grow together in your vision, understanding, and worship of Jesus, the risen and reigning King.

Each day we will offer you a variety of ideas for how your family can worship Jesus and experience His Word together. Review the ideas for each day and choose the ones that best fit your family. Make improvements. Skip some. Add your own new ideas. You know what will work best for your family each day.

We believe this week has the power to transform your home. This might be one of the best weeks your family has spent together in a long time. It will require some planning on your part. The journey begins on Sunday afternoon and ends on

Thursday evening. Look ahead and try to block off about twenty minutes each day for this special time as a family.

HOW TO USE THE FAMILY WORSHIP GUIDE

This guide will help your family come together for five consecutive days of family worship—all with the focus of discovering who King Jesus *really* is. Sunday is different from the other four days in that it introduces your family to the week, and it also includes a special project.

Then Monday through Thursday you will find a suggested plan for daily family worship. Each family worship time has five suggested components: (1) activity, (2) singing, (3) Scripture reading, (4) discussion, and (5) prayer. It is important for the parent or older child who will be leading the family worship time to read the plan for each day ahead of time.

ACTIVITY

If time permits, start with something fun. These activities range from crafts, to games, to object lessons. They usually require little or no preparation. Feel free to adjust and adapt the activity to fit your family. If you have teenagers, encourage them to take the opportunity to lead the activity for the younger kids.

SINGING

Did you say singing? One of the ways God invites us to worship Him is by singing. Jesus, King of the universe, loves to hear us sing to Him!

If your children are younger, and you are enthusiastic about singing, they will love it too. You will lay the groundwork for singing in your family for generations to come. If your kids are all teenagers and you have never tried singing together as a family, do not be afraid to try. If you do not know the songs we recommend, use the Internet to find the lyrics. Just type the song title into your favorite search engine. Do you know other worship songs that honor King Jesus? Sing them with your family.

SCRIPTURE READING

Each family worship time will focus on a particular passage in Scripture. This is the most important part of family worship. Jesus uses His Word to transform us!

DISCUSSION

After each Scripture reading you will find a series of questions that will help your family dig into the truth of God's Word and apply it. Choose the questions you think will work well for your family. Modify the questions as needed.

PRAYER

End your family worship time with prayer. This guide will help your family learn to pray according to the ACTS model.

Adoration, telling Jesus how wonderful He is.

Confession, admitting our sins to God.

Thanksgiving, expressing our gratitude to God.

Supplication, asking God for things we need.

May God the Father richly bless your family this week as you join together in worshipping His Son Jesus, the reigning King!

Richard Ross and Rob Rienow

SUNDAY

HIS THRONE IN YOUR HOME

INTRODUCTION

Today serves as an introduction to the four special days of family worship ahead. If helpful, use the words in bold to help lead your time of family worship. Let the family know you would like them to join you for approximately twenty minutes. Tell them you want to tell them about something special you will be doing together as a family during the week ahead.

This is going to be a special week for our family. Let me tell you about it. I would like to begin with a question. Can anyone tell me what we celebrate on Easter?

Listen to the responses.

That's right, Easter is the day we celebrate Jesus' resurrection from the dead. But did you know that more things happened after Jesus

was raised from the dead? In fact, forty days after Jesus came back to life, He did something very important. Does anyone know what that something was?

Be patient in waiting for an answer, though it is likely that no one will know the answer.

Well, it happened on a Thursday, exactly forty days after Jesus rose from the dead. All His disciples were gathered around Him, and then something incredible happened. Jesus floated up off the ground, went up through the clouds, and He went to be with His Father in heaven! We call this the *ascension* of Christ because the word *ascended* means "to go up."

Unfortunately, we do not talk about the ascension of Christ as much as we should. This week we are going to learn all about it, and we may never be the same!

If someone were to ask you, "Who is Jesus?" what would you say?

Consider writing responses from the family on a paper or a three-by-five-inch card. Don't provide too much help here. Just let the family members offer some of their answers to the question and write them down. It will be helpful to save this paper until your family worship time on Thursday.

Good job. You gave some great answers. My prayer is that this week everyone in our family will become amazed at Jesus' majesty, power, and glory. I am going to ask you this same question on Thursday, and it will not surprise me if you tell me then that Jesus is the triumphant Victor, King of the universe, all-powerful Creator, and supreme Lord of everything! For most of us, our vision and understanding of Jesus are way too small! I believe our vision of who Jesus is will grow this week as we come together and learn more about Jesus, the reigning King.

ACTIVITY

Do you think our family would be different if we recognized that King Jesus is with us in our home every day? Even though we can't see Him

with our eyes, He is here. I am going to need your help with an activity. Because Jesus is the King of kings, we are going to make a throne for Him.

You can do this in a simple way by choosing a chair and decorating it with cloth or colored paper to look like a throne. This should be a chair that you do not usually use at the dinner table. If you want to go all-out, consider building a throne from scratch. Encourage younger children to use their creativity and teens to help their younger siblings.

I imagine you are wondering why we just made a throne. The reason is that this whole week we are going to be thinking about and talking about Jesus as our risen King. Even though we cannot see him, He is alive, and He has more power than any of us can imagine. This throne will remind us that Jesus is the King and that He is present with us.

During all of our meals, the throne will be one of the seats at our table. It will remind us that King Jesus is with us as we eat. Do you think we will treat one another differently with the reminder that Jesus is with us?

Whenever we watch TV this week, we will bring the throne near the TV. When we watch TV, do you think Jesus is present with us?

Yes.

Jesus is always present, but our throne will give us a visible reminder that the King of the universe is watching the same TV shows we are. Do you think having Jesus' throne with us will change what we watch? We will find out.

We will do the same thing when we use the computer. If you want to use a computer or play video games, just pull up the throne! Jesus is with you.

Here is the plan for the week. Each day, from Monday through Thursday, we will set aside some time to get together for a great time of family worship, and we will discover more of who Jesus *really* is.

PRAYER

Would someone be willing to pray and ask God to make this a special week for our family by showing us more of who Jesus really is?

If no one wants to pray, a parent may finish this time in prayer. You might pray words like these.

Dear God,

Thank you for giving us this important family time today. Please make this a special week in our home. As we see this throne we have made, remind us that King Jesus is here with us. Help us do everything in this house to please Him.

Help every one of us during these next few days to grow closer to one another and closer to you. There is so much of who Jesus is that we have not yet discovered. Help us to worship King Jesus with all our hearts.

In the name of Jesus, King of kings and Lord of lords, we pray, Amen.

MONDAY

KING JESUS
CREATES THE UNIVERSE

ACTIVITY

Words in **bold** are what you can say to lead this activity. If you have a mix of teens and younger children, encourage the teens to lead this part of the family worship time.

Supplies needed: (1) a cup of water, (2) 8–10 pillows, (3) 8–10 apples or tennis balls (anything round that is the size of a piece of fruit). You may create your own ideas for supplies after reading the activity instructions.

This is our first special time of family worship this week. To get things started, we have a family challenge. The challenge will be to see how much you can "hold together." I need someone to get a bunch of pillows—as many pillows as you can find.

When all the pillows are collected, **Who wants to volunteer for our first challenge?**

Here is your challenge: Hold as many pillows together in your hands as you can. When we start, someone will hand you a single pillow. Then we will give you a second pillow. Then a third. You have to hold the pillows together in your hands. You cannot hug them. You cannot stack them on your head. How many do you think you can hold together in your hands? Are you ready?

Hand the volunteer the first pillow. Keep adding pillows to see how many pillows he or she can hold together. Give another person a chance to try.

OK, great job. Now for our next challenge. How many balls (or pieces of fruit) do you think you can hold together in your hands? I need a volunteer to try. Remember, you cannot use your arms, just your hands.

Hand the volunteer the first ball (or piece of fruit), then keep giving more until he or she can no longer hold them all together. Give another person a chance to try this challenge if he or she desires.

Time for our final challenge. For this one we need to go to the kitchen sink. We have tried to hold together pillows and balls. I now want you to hold together water. That's right. I want to you to hold water together. Who will volunteer? Gather the family around the sink. **OK, put your hands out over the sink. I will pour this cup of water into your hands, and your job is to hold as much water together as you can.**

Pour the water and see how much they can hold. Not much! Give others a chance to try.

All of you did a great job with our challenge. I want you to remember how hard it was to hold a lot of things together. We are going to talk more about that in a few minutes.

SINGING

Consider one or more of the following songs to praise God for His holiness. Check out www.seedsfamilyworship.com for more ideas.

Hymn: A Mighty Fortress Is Our God
Praise song: We Want to See Jesus Lifted High

SCRIPTURE READING

Choose someone from the family to read the Scripture passage below. If a child is reading, be sure to encourage his or her effort.

Colossians 1:15–20

TALK ABOUT IT

Discuss the following questions as a family. The brief answers provided may help you guide the conversation as needed.

1. Some people think of Jesus as a nice man, a good teacher, or maybe even a prophet. In these five verses, we learn that Jesus is infinitely more. Let us look at these verses again. What are some of the amazing things that we learn about who Jesus really is?

Jesus is the image of the invisible God. To see Jesus is to see God. He is the Creator of all things. He existed before creation. He holds everything together. He is the head of the church. He is the first to be resurrected. In everything He is supreme. He has brought salvation through His blood shed on the cross.

2. According to verse 16, where was Jesus all the way back in Genesis 1:1, at the time of creation? What was He doing?

God did not "make" Jesus when Jesus was born as a baby to Mary and Joseph. He existed long before that. He was there all the way back in Genesis 1:1. Not only was Jesus there, but according to this verse Jesus, as God Himself, created the world!

3. What about before Genesis 1:1? Where was Jesus before the creation of the world?

This will blow your mind! Jesus existed before the universe was made; after all, He created it! Jesus existed before time was made. Think about that for a minute: Jesus existed before time! The truth is that Jesus, as the second person of the Trinity, has always existed.

4. Jesus existed before the universe was created. He created the universe, but what is He doing with His creation now? Let us look at the end of verse 17.

It says, "In him all things hold together" (ESV). Not only did Jesus create the universe, but His power holds it together. If Jesus did not exist right now, neither would you and neither would anything! Jesus made the world and everything in it, and He sustains the world and everything in it.

How did you do holding things together in the activity we did a few minutes ago? We can hold a few things together, but not very much. Every single cell, molecule, and atom in the entire universe is being held together right now by our risen Lord, Jesus Christ!

5. We can learn a lot about who Jesus really is in these verses, but let us look at just one more. Would someone read the last part of verse 18 for us? After someone reads it, ask, **Here we find an amazing word that describes Jesus: Preeminent! (Other translations may say**

supreme.) What does it mean that Jesus is preeminent (supreme) over all things?

(Consider asking someone to look up the definition of the word used in your Bible translation.)

Not only did Jesus create the world, and not only does He keep everything together, but He is supreme over everything! He is supreme over the church. He is supreme over our family. He is supreme over every government. He is supreme over me and over you.

6. How might it change our family if when we thought about Jesus we thought of Him as the Creator, Sustainer, and the one who is supreme over all things in heaven and on earth?

Listen to each person's response.

PRAYER

A powerful way to pray as a family is to follow ACTS.

Adoration, telling Jesus how wonderful He is.
Confession, admitting our sins to God.
Thanksgiving, expressing our gratitude to God.
Supplication, asking God for things we need.

You may choose to pray through one or all of these sections. Invite anyone who wants to pray aloud to do so.

Adoration

In reading the Bible today, what are some of the things we learned about who Jesus really is? He is the Creator and Sustainer of the universe. He is supreme over everything and everyone. Let us take time now and pray and worship Jesus for who He is.

Confession

What sins do we need to confess? Jesus is supreme over every area of our lives. He calls us to be holy. Unfortunately, we all fall short. We all sin. Thankfully, Jesus Himself made a way for us to be forgiven. He loves to hear us pray and confess our sins to Him.

Thanksgiving

We have so much to thank Jesus for! We exist because He made us and continues to "hold us together." Let us pray now and thank Jesus for all He has done for us.

Supplication

Present your requests to God. Ask God to help everyone in your family discover who Jesus really is and worship Him with all their hearts.

A parent can conclude the family worship time with a prayer of thanks to God.

HIS THRONE IN YOUR HOME

Remember to set up your throne for family meals and in front of the TV and computer. Look for opportunities throughout the day to talk about the difference it makes to be reminded that King Jesus is present with you.

BONUS: FAMILY MEMORY VERSE

Consider memorizing this verse together as a family. You might practice it together during mealtimes, e-mail or text it to one another during the day, or talk about it while you drive.

Colossians 1:17 (ESV), "He is before all things, and in him all things hold together."

TUESDAY

KING JESUS FREES US FROM SIN

ACTIVITY

Words in **bold** are what you can say to help lead this activity.

Supplies needed: None

We are going to start family worship with a game. To get started, I need two volunteers— one to be a bad guy and the other to be a prisoner. For families with two people, one person needs to be "the bad guy," and they can take an object "hostage," such as a favorite toy.

OK, our bad guy is not allowed to hurt the prisoner, but we do need you to take your prisoner away to another room in the house. You will need to wait there for about five minutes while the rest of us come up with our plan to help set the prisoner free.

After the prisoner (or object) is taken to another room, the rest of the family members need to decide what they will offer to "the bad guy" as a ransom. If you are a family of three, the remaining person will do the next section on his or her own.

(Talking to the remaining family members) **Well, our dear _____ (name of prisoner) has been taken hostage. It is our job to offer _____ (the bad guy) something that is valuable enough that he/she will be willing to accept it as a ransom payment and let our dear _____ go free. What could we possibly offer?**

You have to come up with real things you can offer. For instance, you cannot offer "this bag filled with $10 million in cash." Find real things you have around the house such as jewelry, favorite toys, money, etc. You only get one chance to make an offer, so make it your best. When you are ready to make the offer, take the items (the ones you can carry) and see if "the bad guy" will make the trade.

If he or she says yes, then the hostage is free! If he or she says no, then the hostage remains in bondage. (It is all pretend, of course. Your bad guy volunteer does not really get the loot and the hostage is released.) Either way the game is finished. You can bring everyone back together.

It is one thing to play this game of prisoner and ransom for fun, but this sometimes happens in real life. Believe it or not, the Bible tells us that we are prisoners because of our sin and we need to be saved! King Jesus is the One who saves us. We will talk about that in a few minutes.

SINGING

Consider one or more of the following songs to praise Jesus for the forgiveness He alone offers to us. Feel free to choose different worship songs your family knows. Use any Internet search engine to find lyrics for the songs below.

Hymn: Lead On, O King Eternal
Praise song: Before the Throne of God Above

SCRIPTURE READING

We are going to read three passages of Scripture today as we discuss how King Jesus made a way for us to be forgiven of our sins.

If possible, encourage three family members to read these verses:

Hebrews 7:27
Hebrews 9:15
Matthew 20:28

TALK ABOUT IT

Discuss the following questions as a family. The brief answers provided may help you guide the conversation as needed.

1. Hebrews 7:27 talks about how Old Testament priests had to offer sacrifices, over and over again, as a symbol of the people's repentance and forgiveness. Why did Jesus have to die only once instead of over and over again to pay for our sins?

A goat is not important enough or valuable enough to pay the price for our sins, let alone for all the sins of all the people who have ever lived. Only Jesus, God Himself, who never sinned, was valuable enough to pay for all our sins, once for all.

2. In Matthew 20:28, Jesus tells us that He came to give His life as a ransom for many. Can you tell me what a ransom is?

Often when a terrorist or criminal takes hostages, he demands to be paid a ransom in order to let the hostages go free. We learned that in the game we played.

3. If Jesus was the ransom, who was "the bad guy," and who were the "hostages"?

"The bad guy" is Satan. In 1 John 5:19 we learn that because of our sin the whole world is under the control of the evil one. We were the hostages—in bondage to sin, death, and Satan.

4. How is it possible that Jesus was able to pay the price for the sins of billions of people?

The answer has to do with who Jesus really is. He is not just a nice man, a good teacher, or a prophet. Do you remember what we learned yesterday? King Jesus is the Creator, Sustainer, and supreme Ruler of the universe. No one else is valuable enough to pay for our sins. Only the sacrifice of the God-man Jesus Christ was a big enough ransom to set us free from sin and death. Jesus took our place on the cross and received the wrath of God the Father against sin—the wrath we deserve. Praise Jesus for His infinite love for us!

5. Some people believe they sin too much or that their sin is too big to be forgiven. Have you ever asked God to forgive you for the same sin, over and over again? Do you ever wonder if God's forgiveness will "run out"?

It is helpful for a parent to be the first to share their struggles with sin and forgiveness. Use this time to encourage your family that if they ever feel like they are "too bad" to be forgiven they are wrong. They are not wrong about how serious their sin is, but they are wrong about Jesus. They have underestimated King Jesus!

Jesus was valuable enough to pay the price for all your sins—past, present, and future. He suffered fully and completely the penalty for our sins. No more work needs to be done! By grace we can always come to Him in faith, confess our sins, and receive forgiveness.

PRAYER

A powerful way to pray as a family is to follow **ACTS.**

Adoration, telling Jesus how wonderful He is.
Confession, admitting our sins to God.
Thanksgiving, expressing our gratitude to God.
Supplication, asking God for things we need.

You may choose to pray through one or all of these sections. Invite anyone who wants to pray aloud to do so.

Adoration

In reading the Bible today, what are some of the things we learned about who Jesus really is? He is a worthy ransom. He is valuable enough to pay for all our sins. Let us praise Jesus for all that He is!

Confession

What sins do we need to confess? No matter what we have done or how many times we have done it, if, by the grace of God, we truly repent and trust Christ alone for forgiveness, we can experience His forgiveness and be restored in our relationship with God. Let us use this time to confess our sins to Jesus and thank Him for His forgiveness. (It is important for a parent to begin this by humbly confessing his or her sin. Kids can then follow your lead.)

Thanksgiving

We have so much to thank Jesus for! Can you imagine being a hostage and the gratitude you would feel toward the one who was willing to trade himself to set you free? Tell Jesus how thankful you are for Him and for all He suffered to save you from your sin.

Supplication

Present your requests to God. God cares about all your needs. Ask God to help everyone in your family discover who Jesus really is and worship Him with all their hearts.

A parent can conclude the family worship time with a prayer of thanks to God.

HIS THRONE IN YOUR HOME

Remember to set your throne up for family meals and in front of the TV and computer. Look for opportunities throughout the day to talk about the difference it makes to be reminded that King Jesus is present with you.

BONUS: FAMILY MEMORY VERSE

Consider memorizing this verse together as a family. You might practice it together during mealtimes, e-mail or text it to one another during the day, or talk about it while you drive.

Matthew 20:28 (ESV), "The Son of Man came not to be served but to serve, and to give his life as a ransom for many."

WEDNESDAY

KING JESUS CONQUERS EVIL

ACTIVITY

Words in **bold** are what you can say to lead this activity. Adapt the activity as you see fit based on the ages of your children. If you have both teens and younger children, encourage the teens to lead the activity. It is good leadership practice for them, and the younger siblings will enjoy it.

Supplies needed: Pen and paper to play a few games of tic-tac-toe

It has been good to have these special times of family worship this week. Every day we have been growing in our understanding of who Jesus really is, and I hope, as that has happened, we have a greater desire to love Him and obey Him.

To start today's family worship time, we are going to have a competition. It is one of the simplest games ever invented. You have probably played it before—maybe on a long, boring car trip. The game is tic-tac-toe.

Get out the paper and pens.

We need two volunteers for our first game. Who wants to play?

Direct volunteers to get ready to play and choose who will be X and who will be O.

Before you start, I need to put in a little twist. First, the player who wins gets to keep playing the next round. You keep facing new opponents until you lose.

Here is the second twist, the person who is X always gets to mark two X marks for every turn. That's right, instead of filling in one X in one space, and then allowing O to go, the X player gets to fill in two spaces.

Make sure the players understand the rules and let the games begin! If all goes according to plan, X will win every game. Play a few rounds, and it will get rather boring. X wins. X wins. X wins.

The competition is not very exciting this way, is it? We know who will win every game. Why? Because the X player, who gets two moves, always has an advantage.

In our family worship time, we are going to talk about the greatest competition in the entire universe—the battle between good and evil. But it is kind of like our game. It is not fair. Satan is on one side and King Jesus is on the other. Satan and God are not equals! Satan has no chance. He never has.

SINGING

Consider one or more of the following songs to praise God for His faithfulness. Use the resources in the introduction to find music and lyrics for suggested songs.

Hymn: All Hail the Power of Jesus' Name
Praise song: Days of Elijah

SCRIPTURE READING

Read the following Scripture out loud as a family. Has one person been doing most of the reading? Consider giving someone else an opportunity.

Colossians 2:13–15

TALK ABOUT IT

Discuss the following questions as a family. The brief answers provided may help you guide the conversation as needed.

1. Verses 13–14 celebrate again what Jesus did for us on the cross by paying the full price for our sins. He cancelled them and took them away. But Jesus did more than take away our personal sins. What does verse 15 say that Jesus also did?

God, in Jesus, disarmed the rulers and authorities (Satan and his demons) and put them

to open shame, triumphing over them by Jesus'
death on the cross. Jesus is not just "our
personal Savior." He conquered all sin, all death,
the devil, and his demons.

2. How did Jesus win the battle against Satan?

Through His resurrection! Satan thought he got
what he wanted when Jesus died on the cross.
He did not know that God had planned to raise
His Son from the dead!

**3. The first time King Jesus came, He came as a
lamb. His death and resurrection won the
decisive battle against Satan. But the war is not
over. The Bible tells us that Jesus is coming
back again, not as a lamb but as a lion. On
Palm Sunday Jesus entered Jerusalem on a
donkey. Next time He will come on a war horse!
Will someone read about the time when Jesus
comes back in Revelation 19:11–16?**

Can you imagine this day? Here Jesus is called
"Faithful and True." He leads the army of
warrior angels against the forces of evil gathered
against Him. On His thigh is written this name:

"King of kings and Lord of lords." Do you know how Jesus wins this battle? In 2 Thessalonians God tells us that Jesus wins this giant battle with the breath of His mouth! One breath and it is over. Now that is ultimate power!

4. When you think about Jesus, do you think about Him as a great warrior, leading the armies of heaven, or only as a gentle teacher?

Listen to the responses.

5. If Jesus has conquered sin, death, and the devil, what difference does that make in how we resist sin and seek to obey God?

King Jesus has won the victory. The battle is His, not ours. This means that if, by the grace of God, we have repented of our sins and trusted Christ as Lord, this same King Jesus resides in our hearts, and even more importantly the Bible says that we now live *in Him*. When we are tempted to sin (talk about what some of those temptations are for your family), we do not have to use our own willpower to make the right decision. In that moment we can pray to King

Jesus and ask Him to fight that battle for us. In that moment, we can choose to live in Christ, knowing that He has already won the victory over that sin.

PRAYER

We will again follow the ACTS prayer model.

Adoration, telling Jesus how wonderful He is.
Confession, admitting our sins to God.
Thanksgiving, expressing our gratitude to God.
Supplication, asking God for things we need.

You may choose to pray through one or all of these sections. Invite anyone who wants to pray aloud to do so.

Adoration

In reading the Bible today, what are some of the things we learned about King Jesus? We learned that Jesus conquered all the forces of evil through His resurrection from the dead. He promises that He is coming back again for the final battle. Let us pray now and worship King Jesus for His victory.

Confession

King Jesus takes sin and evil seriously. He takes sin in our lives seriously. Thankfully, we can confess our sins to Him. Because of His love for us and His victory over evil, He is able to forgive us. Let us confess our sins aloud to Jesus right now.

It is helpful for a parent to begin this time.

Thanksgiving

Does knowing that Jesus has fought the battle against evil and won make you thankful? Does knowing that Jesus will return to make everything right and bring glory to His Father make you thankful? Does knowing you can have hope, even in the middle of the saddest times of your life, make you thankful? Thank Him for these things.

Supplication

If we are going to battle sin in our lives, we need to rely on King Jesus, who has already won! Let us use this time to ask Jesus to fight against sin in our lives.

A parent can say a brief prayer to conclude your time of family worship.

HIS THRONE IN YOUR HOME

Remember to set your throne up for family meals and in front of the TV and computer. Look for opportunities throughout the day to talk about the difference it makes to be reminded that King Jesus is present with you.

BONUS: FAMILY MEMORY VERSE

Consider memorizing this verse together as a family. You might practice it together during mealtimes, e-mail or text it to one another during the day, or talk about it while you drive.

Colossians 2:15 (ESV), "[God] disarmed the rulers and authorities and put them to open shame, by triumphing over them in [Jesus]."

THURSDAY

KING JESUS
ASCENDS TO HEAVEN

REFLECT ON THE WEEK

Words in **bold** are what you can say to lead this time of reflection.

Supplies needed: The throne you made and the piece of paper from Sunday on which you wrote your description of Jesus.

Today is the special day that we have been looking forward to all week. Does anyone know what happened forty days after Jesus rose from the dead?

The resurrected Christ ascended into heaven.

Our prayer this week has been that God would show us more of who His Son Jesus really is. On Sunday I asked you to tell me who you thought

Jesus was. Do you remember some of the things you said?

Listen to responses, and refer to the card to help you remember.

We also made this throne. We made it to remind us that King Jesus is present in our home. He is with us when we eat, and when we watch TV. No matter what we are doing, King Jesus is here. Did you see a difference in our family this week because of this reminder that King Jesus is here with us?

Listen to responses. It will be important for a parent to share personally about how focusing on Christ's presence in the home this week made a difference in your heart, attitude, and choices.

Let us look at our paper again with our descriptions of Jesus. In what ways was our view and understanding of Jesus too small? Did we write down who He really is?

We have been reading the Bible together so we could see more of the real Jesus. In light of what

God has shown us, what else should we write down on the paper?

Feel free to skim back over the family worship guide or review the Scriptures you read. Write down additional truths about Jesus on your paper or card.

This is not our last time of family worship, but it is the end of this special week. Let us worship Jesus together and then read about what happened on that special day, forty days after Jesus' resurrection.

SINGING

Consider one or more of the following songs to praise Jesus. For older kids and teens that play an instrument, encourage them to learn a song in advance to be able to add their gift of music to the family worship time.

Hymn: 'Tis So Sweet to Trust in Jesus
Praise song: Holy and Anointed One

The first few times you try and sing together may be awkward. Do not give up! God loves it.

SCRIPTURE READING

Read the following Scriptures out loud as a family. Does one person usually read the Bible during this time? Consider asking someone else to read today.

Acts 1:1–11 (We will also read Hebrews 1:1–3 in a few moments.)

TALK ABOUT IT

Discuss the following questions as a family. The brief answers provided may help you guide the conversation as needed.

1. How do you think the disciples felt watching Jesus rise up into the clouds and out of sight?

Listen to the responses. Think about the highs (Jesus' ministry with them), the lows (His death) and the super-highs (His resurrection) the disciples experienced.

2. Where did Jesus go after He went up through the clouds?

God answers this in the book of Hebrews. Let us go there and see what Hebrews 1:1–3 says. In these three verses we will see a lot of the amazing things about King Jesus that we have been talking about all week, and we will also learn where Jesus went.

Read Hebrews 1:1–3 aloud.

3. What about King Jesus from Hebrews 1:1–3 have we already learned this week?

King Jesus made the universe. He is the exact representation of God. When we see Jesus, we see God. He sustains all things; in other words He holds all things together. He provided purification for sins. Jesus is the only one who could do the work, and who did do the work, to save us.

4. According to the end of verse 3, where did Jesus go when He ascended into heaven?

He sat down at the right hand of the Father. God the Father gave to God the Son the greatest place of honor, power, and authority.

5. Many people, when they talk about Jesus, talk about Him like a friend. They talk about their "personal relationship with Jesus." They talk about how "Jesus helps them when they need Him." These things are all true. Jesus is our friend. We can have a personal relationship with Him. Jesus does help us when we need Him. But if we are not careful, we can start to treat Jesus like a pal or a good-luck charm. We live our lives, we do what we want, and Jesus is along for our ride.

This week we learned more about who Jesus really is. How would each of us as individuals, and how would our family, be different if every day we believed in, obeyed, and worshipped Jesus as the King of kings and Lord of lords?

Take time to listen to the responses. It is helpful for a parent to share humbly the ways Jesus has changed him/her during this week.

PRAYER

Once again we will conclude our family worship time using the ACTS prayer model.

Adoration, telling Jesus how wonderful He is.
Confession, admitting our sins to God.
Thanksgiving, expressing our gratitude to God.
Supplication, asking God for things we need.

You may choose to pray through one or all of these sections. Invite anyone who wants to pray aloud to do so.

Adoration

In reading the Bible today, what are some of the things we learned about King Jesus? He miraculously ascended to heaven forty days after His resurrection. He promises that He will come back again. Right now Jesus is seated in majesty at the right hand of Father God. Worship Jesus for these things.

Confession

King Jesus knows all our sins and has made one and only one way to be forgiven. That one way is Himself! The grace of God enables us to repent and put our faith in Jesus. Walking with Jesus is a continual journey of repenting and believing. Let us repent of our sins together now. (Parent, be the first to confess. It helps the kids follow your lead.)

Thanksgiving

Thank Jesus for His goodness and mercy. Thank Him for never giving up on His children. Thank Him for preparing for us a perfect life on a brand-new earth, which will last forever! Thank Him for this special week of family worship. Thank Him for promising to return again.

Supplication

Ask God to give you a growing understanding and vision of the majesty and glory of His Son Jesus. Ask God that your family would never forget and always live according to the truth that His throne is in your home.

A parent can close the time of family worship in prayer. Consider taking extra time to celebrate your family's spiritual journey this week. Go out for ice cream. Take a walk. Do something that is a special treat.

BONUS: FAMILY MEMORY VERSE

Consider memorizing this verse together as a family. You might practice it together during mealtimes, e-mail or text it to one another during the day, or talk about it while you drive.

Hebrews 1:3 (ESV), "He [Jesus] is the radiance of the glory of God and the exact imprint of his nature, and he upholds the universe by the word of his power. After making purification for sins, he sat down at the right hand of the Majesty on high."

DO NOT STOP NOW!

We pray that God has used this week to turn your hearts toward King Jesus and toward one another. We pray He has done this to transform your home for the glory of God the Father and His Son Jesus Christ. We encourage you to maintain your commitment to making family worship the centerpiece of your family's life together.

All for Jesus,

Richard Ross and Rob Rienow

"Love the LORD your God with all your heart and with all your soul and with all your might. And these words that I command you today shall be on your heart. You shall teach them diligently to your children, and shall talk of them when you sit in your house."
—Deuteronomy 6:5-7 (ESV)

Written and copyrighted by Rob Rienow and Richard Ross

Use the web sites below to discover more family-equipping books and resources or to learn more about inviting Richard Ross or Rob Rienow to speak at your church or ministry event.

Richard Ross, www.richardaross.com

Rob Rienow, www.VisionaryFam.com